A New and Comprehensive Vocabulary of the Flash Language

James Hardy Vaux

ORIGINAL DEDICATION.

To THOMAS SKOTTOWE, Esq., of His Majesty's 73d Regiment, Commandant of Newcastle, in the Colony of New South Wales, and one of His Majesty's Justices of the Peace for that Territory.

SIR,

WITH the utmost deference and respect, I beg leave to submit to your perusal the following sheets. The idea of such a compilation first originated in the suggestion of a friend; and however the theme may be condemned as exceptionable by narrow minds, I feel confident you possess too much liberality of sentiment to reject its writer as utterly depraved, because he has acquired an extensive knowledge on a subject so obviously disgraceful. True it is, that in the course of a chequered and eventful life, I have intermixed with the most dissolute and unprincipled characters, and that a natural quickness of conception, and most retentive memory, have rendered me familiar with their language and system of operations.

Permit me, Sir, to assure you most seriously, that I view with remorse the retrospect of my hitherto misspent life, and that my future exertions shall be solely directed to acquire the estimable good opinion of the virtuous part of the community.

I trust the Vocabulary will afford you some amusement from its novelty; and that from the correctness of its definitions, you may occasionally find it useful in your magisterial capacity.

I cannot omit this opportunity of expressing my gratitude for the very humane and equitable treatment I have experienced in common with every other person in this settlement, under your temperate and judicious government.

I have the honour to remain, with the most dutiful respect, Sir, Your devoted, and very humble Servant,

J. H. VAUX.

Newcastle,
5th July, 1812.

The Author (a prisoner under sentence of transportation for life) having, by an alleged act of impropriety, incurred the Governor's displeasure, was at this period banished to Newcastle, a place of punishment for offenders: these sheets were there compiled during his solitary hours of cessation from hard labour; and the Commandant was accordingly presented by the Author with the first copy of his production.

A New and Comprehensive Vocabulary of the Flash Language

A VOCABULARY OF THE FLASH LANGUAGE

ALDERMAN LUSHINGTON. See LUSH.

ANDREW MILLER'S LUGGER: a king's ship or vessel.

AREA SNEAK, or AREA SLUM: the practice of slipping unperceived down the areas of private houses, and robbing the lower apartments of plate or other articles.

ARM-PITS: To work under the arm-pits, is to practise only such kinds of depredation, as will amount, upon conviction, to what the law terms single, or petty larceny; the extent of punishment for which is transportation for seven years. By following this system, a thief avoids the halter, which certainly is applied above the arm-pits.

AWAKE: an expression used on many occasions; as a thief will say to his accomplice, on perceiving the person they are about to rob is aware of their intention, and upon his guard, stow it, the cove's awake. To be awake to any scheme, deception, or design, means, generally, to see through or comprehend it.

BACK-JUMP. A back-window. See JUMP.

BACK-SLANG: to enter or come out of a house by the back-door; or, to go a circuitous or private way through the streets, in order to avoid any particular place in the direct road, is termed back-slanging it.

BACK-SLUM: a back room; also the back entrance to any house or premises; thus, we'll give it 'em on the back-slum, means, we'll get in at the back-door.

BAD HALFPENNY. When a man has been upon any errand, or attempting any object which has proved unsuccessful or impracticable, he will say on his return, It's a bad halfpenny; meaning he has returned as he went.

BANDED: hungry.

BANDS. To wear the bands, is to be hungry, or short of food for any length of time; a phrase chiefly used on board the hulks, or in jails.

A New and Comprehensive Vocabulary of the Flash Language

BANG- UP. A person, whose dress or equipage is in the first style of perfection, is declared to be bang up to the mark. A man who has behaved with extraordinary spirit and resolution in any enterprise he has been engaged in, is also said to have come bang up to the mark; any article which is remarkably good or elegant, or any fashion, act, or measure which is carried to the highest pitch, is likewise illustrated by the same emphatical phrase.

BARKING-IRONS: pistols; an obsolete term.

BARNACLES: spectacles.

BASH: to beat any person by way of correction, as the woman you live with, etc.

BASTILE: generally called, for shortness, the Steel; a cant name for the House of Correction, Cold-Bath-Fields, London.

BEAK: a magistrate; the late Sir John Fielding, of police memory, was known among family people by the title of the blind beak.

BEAN: a guinea.

BEEF: stop thief! to beef a person, is to raise a hue and cry after him, in order to get him stopped.

BELLOWSER. See WIND.

BENDER: a sixpence.

BENDER: an ironical word used in conversation by flash people; as where one party affirms or professes any thing which the other believes to be false or insincere, the latter expresses his incredulity by exclaiming bender! or, if one asks another to do any act which the latter considers unreasonable or impracticable, he replies, O yes, I'll do it—bender; meaning, by the addition of the last word, that, in fact, he will do no such thing.

BEST: to get your money at the best, signifies to live by dishonest or fraudulent practices, without labour or industry, according to the general acceptation of the latter word; but, certainly, no persons have more occasion to be industrious, and in a state of perpetual action than cross-coves; and experience has proved, when too late, to many

A New and Comprehensive Vocabulary of the Flash Language

of them, that honesty is the best policy; and, consequently, that the above phrase is by no means a-propos.

BETTY: picklock; to unbetty, or b e g a lock, to open or relock it, by means of the betty, so as to avoid subsequent detection.

BILLIARD SLUM. The mace is sometimes called giving it to 'em on the billiard slum. See MACE.

BISHOP. See CHRISTEN.

BIT: money in general.

BIT-FAKER: a coiner. See FAKE.

BIT-FAKING: coining base money.

BLACK DIAMONDS: coals.

BLEEDERS: spurs.

BLOODY-JEMMY: a sheep's head.

BLOW THE GAFF: a person having any secret in his possession, or a knowledge of any thing injurious to another, when at last induced from revenge, or other motive, to tell it openly to the world and expose him publicly, is then said to have blown the gaff upon him.

BLOWEN: a prostitute; a woman who cohabits with a man without marriage.

BLUE-PIGEON: lead.

BLUE-PIGEON FLYING: the practice of stealing lead from houses, churches, or other buildings, very prevalent in London and its vicinity.

BLUNT: money.

BOB, or BOBSTICK: a shilling.

BODY-SLANGS. See SLANGS.

A New and Comprehensive Vocabulary of the Flash Language

BODY-SNATCHER: a stealer of dead bodies from church which are sold to the surgeons and students in anatomy.

BOLT: to run. away from or leave any place suddenly, is c bolting, or making a bolt: a thief observing an alarm while attempting a robbery, will exclaim to his accomplice, Bolt, there's a dawn. sudden escape of one or more prisoners from a place of confinement is termed a bolt.

BOLT-IN-TURN: a term founded on the cant word bolt merely a fanciful variation, very common among flash persons, there being in London a famous inn so called; it is customary when a man has run away from his lodgings, broke out of a jail, or ma any other sudden movement, to say, The Bolt-in-fun is concerned; or? He's gone to the Bolt-in-turn; instead of simply saying, He has bolted, etc. See BOLT.

BONED: taken in custody, apprehended; Tell us how you was boned, signifies, tell us the story of your apprehension; a common request among fellow-prisoners in a jail, etc., which is readily complied with in general; and the various circumstances therein related afford present amusement, and also useful hints for regulating their future operations, so as to avoid the like misfortune.

BONNET: a concealment, pretext, or pretence; an ostensible manner of accounting for what you really mean to conceal; as a man who actually lives by depredation, will still outwardly follow some honest employment, as a clerk, porter, newsman, etc. By this system of policy, he is said to have a good bonnet if he happens to get boned, and, in a doubtful case, is commonly discharged on the score of having a good character. To bonnet for a person, is to corroborate any assertion he has made, or to relate facts in the most favourable light, in order to extricate him from a dilemma, or to further any object he has in view.

BOUNCE: to bully, threaten, talk loud, or affect great consequence; to bounce a person out of any thing, is to use threatening or high words, in order to intimidate him, and attain the object you are intent upon; or to obtain goods of a tradesman, by assuming the appearance of great respectability and importance, so as to remove any suspicion he might at first entertain. A thief, detected in the commission of a robbery, has been known by this sort of finesse, aided by a genteel appearance and polite manners, to persuade his accusers of his innocence, and not only to get off with a good grace,

A New and Comprehensive Vocabulary of the Flash Language

but induce them to apologize for their supposed mistake, and the affront put upon him. This masterstroke of effrontery is called giving it to 'em upon the bounce.

BOUNCE: a person well or fashionably drest, is said to be a rank bounce.

BOWLED OUT: a man who has followed the profession of thieving for some time, when he is ultimately taken, tried, and convicted, is said to be bowled out at last. To bowl a person out, in a general sense, means to detect him in the commission of any fraud, or peculation, which he has hitherto practised without discovery.

BRACE UP: to dispose of stolen goods by pledging them for the utmost you can get at a pawnbroker's, is termed bracing them up.

BRADS: halfpence; also, money in general.

BREAKING UP OF THE SPELL: the nightly termination of performance at the Theatres Royal, which is regularly attended by pickpockets of the lower order, who exercise their vocation about the doors and avenues leading thereto, until the house is emptied and the crowd dispersed.

BREECH'D: flush of money.

BRIDGE: to bridge a person, or throw him over the bridge, is, in a general sense, to deceive him by betraying the confidence he has reposed in you, and instead of serving him faithfully, to involve him in ruin or disgrace; or, three men being concerned alike in any transaction, two of them will form a collusion to bridge the third, and engross to themselves all the advantage which may eventually accrue. Two persons having been engaged in a long and doubtful contest or rivalship, he, who by superior art or perseverance gains the point, is said to have thrown his opponent over the bridge. Among gamblers, it means deceiving the person who had back'd you, by wilfully losing the game; the money so lost by him being shared between yourself and your confederates who had laid against you. In playing three-handed games, two of the party will play into each other's hands, so that the third must inevitably be thrown over the bridge, commonly called, two poll one. See PLAY ACROSS.

A New and Comprehensive Vocabulary of the Flash Language

BROADS: cards; a person expert at which is said to be a good broad-player.

BROOMSTICKS. See QUEER BAIL.

BROWNS and WHISTLERS: bad halfpence and farthings; (a term used by coiners.)

BUB: a low expression signifying drink.

BUCKET. To bucket a person is synonymous with putting him in the well. See WELL. Such treatment is said to be a bucketting concern.

BUFF, To buff a person or thing, is to swear to the identity of them; swearing very positively to any circumstance, is called buffing it home.

BUFFER: a dog.

BUG or BUG OVER. To give, deliver, or hand over; as, He bug'd me a quid, he gave me a guinea; bug over the rag, hand over the money.

BULL: a crown, or five shillings.

BULL-DOG: a sugar-loaf.

BULL-HANKERS: men who delight in the sport of bull-banking; that is, bull-baiting, or bullock-hunting, games which afford much amusement, and at the same time frequent opportunities of depredation, in the confusion and alarm excited by the enraged animal.

BUM-CHARTER: a name given to bread steeped in hot water, by the first unfortunate inhabitants of the English Bastile, where this miserable fare was their daily breakfast, each man receiving with his; scanty portion of bread, a quart of boil'd water from the cook's coppers!

BUM-TRAP: a sheriff's officer or his follower.

BUNCE: money.

BURICK: a prostitute, or common woman.

A New and Comprehensive Vocabulary of the Flash Language

BUSH'D: poor; without money.

BUSHY-PARK: a man who is poor is said to be at Bushy park, or in the park.

BUSTLE: a cant term for money.

BUSTLE: any object effected very suddenly, or in a hurry, is said to be done upon the bustle. To give it to a man upon the bustle, is to obtain any point, as borrowing money, etc. ; by some sudden story or pretence, and affecting great haste, so that he is taken by surprise, and becomes duped before he has time to consider of the matter.

BUZ: to buz a person is to pick his pocket. The buz is the game of picking pockets in general.

BUZ-COVE, or BUZ-GLOAK: a pickpocket; a person who is clever at this practice, is said to be a good buz.

CABIN: a house.

CADGE: to beg. The cadge is the game or profession of begging.

CADGE-CLOAK: a beggar.

CANT OF DOBBIN: a roll of riband.

CAP: synonymous with BONNET, which see.

CARDINAL: a lady's cloak.

CARRY THE KEG: a man who is easily vexed or put out of humour by any joke passed upon him, and cannot conceal his chagrin, is said to carry the keg, or is compared to a walking distiller.

CASTOR: a hat.

CAT and KITTEN RIG: the petty game of stealing pewter quart and pint pots from public-houses.

CAZ: cheese; As good as caz, is a phrase signifying that any projected fraud or robbery may be easily and certainly accomplished; any person who is the object of such attempt and is

A New and Comprehensive Vocabulary of the Flash Language

known to be an easy dupe, is declared to be as good as caz, meaning that success is certain.

CHANDLER-KEN: a chandler's shop.

CHANT: a person's name, address, or designation; thus, a thief who assumes a feigned name on his apprehension to avoid being known, or a swindler who gives a false address to a tradesman, is said to tip them a queer chant.

CHANT: a cipher, initials, or mark of any kind, on a piece of plate, linen, or other article; any thing so marked is said to be chanted.

CHANT: an advertisement in a newspaper or hand-bill; also a paragraph in the newspaper describing any robbery or other recent event; any lost or stolen property, for the recovery of which, or a thief, etc., for whose apprehension a reward is held out by advertisement, are said to be chanted.

CHARLEY: a watchman.

CHARLEY-KEN: a watch-box.

CHATS: lice.

CHATTY: lousy,

CHAUNT: a song; to chaunt is to sing; to throw off a rum chaunt, is to sing a good song.

CHEESE IT. The same as Stow it.

CHEESE THAT. See STOW THAT.

CHINA STREET: a cant name for Bow Street, Covent Garden.

CHIV: a knife; to chiv a person is to stab or cut him with a knife.

CHRISTEN: obliterating the name and number on the movement on a stolen watch; or the crest, cipher, etc., on articles of plate, and getting others engraved, so as to prevent their being identified, is termed having them bishop'd or christen'd.

A New and Comprehensive Vocabulary of the Flash Language

CHUM: a fellow prisoner in a jail, hulk, etc. ; so there are new chums and old chums, as they happen to have been a short or a long time in confinement.

CHURY: a knife.

CLEANED OUT: said of a gambler who has lost his last stake at play; also, of a flat who has been stript of all his money by a coalition of sharps.

CLOUT: a handkerchief of any kind.

CLOUTING: the practice of picking pockets exclusively of handkerchiefs.

CLY: a pocket.

CLY-FAKER: a pickpocket.

COACH-WHEEL: a dollar or crown-piece.

COME. A thief observing any article in a shop, or other situation, which he conceives may be easily purloined, will say to his accomplice, I think there is so and so to come.

COME IT: to divulge a secret; to tell any thing of one party to another; they say of a thief who has turned evidence against his accomplices, that he is coming all he knows, or that he comes it as strong as a horse.

COME TO THE HEATH: a phrase signifying to pay or give money, and synonymous with Tipping, from which word it takes its rise, there being a place called Tiptree Heath, I believe, in the County of Essex.

COME TO THE MARK: to abide strictly by any contract previously made; to perform your part manfully in any exploit or enterprise you engage in; or to offer what I consider a fair price for any article in question.

CONCERNED. In using many cant words, the lovers of flash, by way of variation, adopt this term, for an illustration of which, see BOLT-IN-TURN, ALDERMAN LUSHINGTON, MR. PALMER, etc.

A New and Comprehensive Vocabulary of the Flash Language

CONK: the nose.

CONK: a thief who impeaches his accomplices; a spy; informer, or tell-tale. See NOSE, and WEAR IT.

COVE: the master of a house or shop, is called the Cove; on other occasions, when joined to particular words, as a cross-cove, a flash-cove, a leary-cove, etc., it simply implies a man of these several descriptions; sometimes, in speaking of any third person, whose name you are either ignorant of, or don't wish to mention, the word cove is adopted by way of emphasis, as may be seen under the word AWAKE.

COVER: to stand in such a situation as to obscure your Pall, who is committing a robbery, from the view of by-standers or persons passing, is called covering him. Any body whose dress or stature renders him particularly eligible for this purpose, is said to be a good cover.

COVESS: the mistress of a house or shop, and used on other occasions, in the same manner as Cove, when applied to a man.

CRAB: to prevent the perfection or execution of any intended matter or business, by saying any thing offensive or unpleasant, is called crabbing it, or throwing a crab; to crab a person, is to use offensive language or behaviour as will highly displease, or put him in an ill humour.

CRAB'D: affronted; out of humour; sometimes called, being in Crab-street.

CRABSHELLS: shoes.

CRACK: to break open; the crack is the game of house-breaking; a crack is a breaking any house or building for the purpose of plunder.

CRACKSMAN: a house-breaker.

CRACK A WHID: to speak or utter: as, he crack'd some queer whids, he dropt some bad or ugly expressions: crack a whid for me, intercede, or put in a word for me.

A New and Comprehensive Vocabulary of the Flash Language

CRACKER: a small loaf, served to prisoners in jails, for their daily subsistence.

CRAP: the gallows.

CRAP'D: hanged.

CRIB: a house, sometimes applied to shops, as, a thimble-crib, a watch-maker's shop; a stocking-crib, a hosier's, etc.

CROAK: to die.

CROOK: a sixpence.

CROSS: illegal or dishonest practices in general are called the cross, in opposition to the square. See SQUARE. Any article which has been irregularly obtained, is said to have been got upon the cross, and is emphatically termed a cross article.

CROSS-COVE, or CROSS-MOLLISHER, a man or woman who lives upon the cross.

CROSS-CRIB: a house inhabited, or kept by family people. See SQUARE CRIB.

CROSS-FAM: to cross-fam a person, is to pick his pocket, by crossing your arms in a particular position.

CUE. See letter Q.

CUT THE LINE. See LINE.

CUT THE STRING. See STRING.

CUT THE TARN. See YARN.

CUTTING-GLOAK: a man famous for drawing a knife, and cutting any person he quarrels with.

DAB: a bed. DAB IT UP: to dab it up with a woman, is to agree to cohabit with her.

DANCERS: stairs.

A New and Comprehensive Vocabulary of the Flash Language

DANNA: human, or other excrement.

DANNA-DRAG: commonly pronounced dunnick-drag. See KNAP A JACOB, etc.

DARBIES: fetters.

DARKY: night.

DARKY: a dark lanthorn.

DEATH-HUNTER: an undertaker.

DICKY, or DICK IN THE GREEN: very bad or paltry; any thing of an inferior quality, is said to be a dicky concern.

DIMMOCK: money.

DING: to throw, or throw away; particularly any article you have stolen, either because it is worthless, or that there is danger of immediate apprehension. To ding a person, is to drop his acquaintance totally; also to quit his company, or leave him for the time present; to ding to your pall, is to convey to him, privately, the property you have just stolen; and he who receives it is said to take ding, or to knap the ding.

DINGABLE: any thing considered worthless, or which you can well spare, having no further occasion for it, is declared to be dingable. This phrase is often applied by sharps to a flat whom they have cleaned out; and by abandoned women to a keeper, who having spent his all upon them, must be discarded, or ding'd as soon as possible.

DISPATCHES: false dice used by gamblers, so contrived as always to throw a nick.

DO: a term used by smashers; to do a queer half-quid, or a queer screen, is to utter a counterfeit half-guinea, or a forged bank-note.

DO IT AWAY: to fence or dispose of a stolen article beyond the reach of probable detection.

A New and Comprehensive Vocabulary of the Flash Language

DO IT UP: to accomplish any object you have in view; to obtain any thing you were in quest of, is called doing it up for such a thing; a person who contrives by nob-work, or ingenuity, to live an easy life and appears to improve daily in circumstances, is said to do it up ill good twig.

DO THE TRICK: to accomplish any robbery, or other business successfully; a thief who has been fortunate enough to acquire an independence, and prudent enough to tie it up in time, is said by his former associates to have done the trick; on the other hand, a man who has imprudently involved himself in some great misfortune, from which there is little hope of his extrication is declared by his friends, with an air of commiseration, to have done the trick for himself; that is, his ruin or downfall is nearly certain.

DOBBIN: riband. See CANT.

DOLLOP: a dollop is a large quantity of any thing; the whole dollop means the total quantity.

DONE: convicted; as, he was done for a crack, he was convicted of house-breaking.

DORSE: a lodging; to dorse with a woman, signifies to sleep with her.

DOUBLE: to double a person, or tip him the Dublin packet, signifies either to run away from him openly, and elude his attempts to overtake you, or to give him the slip in the streets, or elsewhere, unperceived, commonly done to escape from an officer who has you in custody, or to turn up a flat of any kind, whom you have a wish to get rid of.

DOUBLE-SLANGS: double-irons.

DOWN: sometimes synonymous with awake, as, when the party you are about to rob, sees or suspects your intention, it is then said that the cove is down. A down is a suspicion, alarm, or discovery, which taking place, obliges yourself and palls to give up or desist from the business or depredation you were engaged in; to put a down upon a man, is to give information of any robbery or fraud he is about to perpetrate, so as to cause his failure or detection; to drop dawn to a person is to discover or be aware of his character or designs; to put a

A New and Comprehensive Vocabulary of the Flash Language

person down to any thing, is to apprize him of, elucidate, or explain it to him; to put a swell down, signifies to alarm or put a gentleman on his guard, when in the attempt to pick his pocket, you fail to effect it at once, and by having touched him a little too roughly, you cause him to suspect your design, and to use precautions accordingly; or perhaps, in the act of sounding him, by being too precipitate or incautious, his suspicions may have been excited, and it is then said that you have put him down, put him fly, or spoiled him. See SPOIL IT. To drop dawn upon yourself, is to become melancholy, or feel symptoms of remorse or compunction, on being committed to jail, cast for death, etc. To sink under misfortunes of any kind. A man who gives way to this weakness, is said to be down upon himself.

DOWN AS A HAMMER; DOWN AS A TRIPPET. These are merely emphatical phrases, used out of flash, to signify being dawn, leary, fly, or awake to any matter, meaning, or design.

DRAG: a cart. The drag, is the game of robbing carts, waggons, or carriages, either in town or country, of trunks, bale-goods, or any other property. Done for a drag, signifies convicted for a robbery of the before-mentioned nature.

DRAG-COVE: the driver of a cart.

DRAGS MAN: a thief who follows the game of dragging.

DRAKED: ducked; a discipline sometimes inflicted on pickpockets at fairs, races, etc.

DRAW: to draw a person, is to pick his pocket, and the act of so stealing a pocket-book, or handkerchief, is called drawing a reader, or clout. To obtain money or goods of a person by a false or plausible story, is called drawing him of so and so. To draw a kid, is to obtain his swag from him. See KID-RIG.

DRIZ: lace, as sold on cards by the haberdashers, etc.

DROP: the game of ring-dropping is called the drop.

DROP: to give or present a person with money, as, he dropp'd me a quid, he gave me a guinea. A kid who delivers his bundle to a sharper without hesitation, or a shopkeeper who is easily duped of

A New and Comprehensive Vocabulary of the Flash Language

his goods by means of a forged order or false pretence, is said to drop the swag in good twig, meaning, to part with it freely.

DROP A WHID: to let fall a word, either inadvertently or designedly.

DROP-COVE: a sharp who practises the game of ring-dropping.

DROP-DOWN. See DOWN.

DRUMMOND: any scheme or project considered to be infallible, or any event which is deemed inevitably certain, is declared to be a Drummond; meaning, it is as sure as the credit of that respectable banking-house, Drummond and Co.

DUB: a key.

DUB AT A KNAPPING-JIGGER: a collector of tolls at a turnpike-gate.

DUB-COVE, or DUBSMAN: a turnkey.

DUBLIN-PACKET. See DOUBLE.

DUB UP: to lock up or secure any thing or place; also to button one's pocket, coat, etc.

DUCE. Twopence is called a duce.

DUDS: women's apparel in general.

DUES. This term is sometimes used to express money, where any certain sum or payment is spoken of; a man asking for money due to him for any service done, or a blowen requiring her previous compliment from a family-man, would say, Come, tip us the dues. So a thief, requiring his share of booty from his palls, will desire them to bring the dues to light.

DUES. This word is often introduced by the lovers of flash on many occasions, but merely out of fancy, and can only be understood from the context of their discourse; like many other cant terms, it is not easily explained on paper; for example, speaking of a man likely to go to jail, one will say, there will be quodding dues concerned, of a

A New and Comprehensive Vocabulary of the Flash Language

man likely to be executed; there will be topping dues, if any thing is alluded to that will require a fee or bribe, there must be tipping dues, or palming dues concerned, etc.

DUMMY: a pocket-book; a silly half-witted person.

DUMMY-HUNTERS: thieves who confine themselves to the practice of stealing gentlemen's pocket-books, and think, or profess to think, it paltry to touch a clout, or other insignificant article; this class of depredators traverse the principal streets of London, during the busy hours, and sometimes meet with valuable prizes.

DUNNICK, or DANNA-DRAG. See KNAP A JACOB.

FADGE: a farthing.

FAKE: a word so variously used, that I can only illustrate it by a few examples. To fake any person or place, may signify to rob them; to fake a person, may also imply to shoot, wound, or cut; to fake a man out and out, is to kill him; a man who inflicts wounds upon, or otherwise disfigures, himself, for any sinister purpose, is said to have faked himself; if a man's shoe happens to pinch, or gall his foot, from its being overtight, he will complain that his shoe fakes his foot sadly; it also describes the doing of any act, or the fabricating any thing, as, to fake your slangs, is to cut your irons in order to escape from custody; to fake your pin, is to create a sore leg, or to cut it, as if accidentally, with an axe, etc., in hopes to obtain a discharge from the army or navy, to get into the doctor's list, etc. ; to fake a screeve, is to write a letter, or other paper; to fake a screw, is to shape out a skeleton or false key, for the purpose of screwing a particular place; to fake a cly, is to pick a pocket; etc., etc., etc.

FAKE AWAY, THERE'S NO DOWN: an intimation from a thief to his pall, during the commission of a robbery, or other act, meaning, go on with your operations, there is no sign of any alarm or detection.

FAKEMAN-CHARLEY; FAKEMENT. As to fake signifies to do any act, or make any thing, so the fakement means the act or thing alluded to, and on which your discourse turns; consequently, any stranger unacquainted with your subject will not comprehend what is meant by the fakement; for instance, having recently been concerned with another in some robbery, and immediately

A New and Comprehensive Vocabulary of the Flash Language

separated, the latter taking the booty with him, on your next meeting you will inquire, what he has done with the fakement? meaning the article stolen, whether it was a pocket-book, piece or linen, or what not. Speaking of any stolen property which has a private mark, one will say, there is a fakeman-charley on it; a forgery which is well executed, is said to be a prime fakement; in a word, any thing is liable to be termed a fakement, or a fakeman-charley, provided the person you address knows to what you allude.

FAM: the hand.

FAM: to feel or handle.

FAMILY: thieves, sharpers and all others who get their living upon the cross, are comprehended under the title of "The Family."

FAMILY-MAN, or WOMAN: any person known or recognised as belonging to the family; all such are termed family people.

FANCY: any article universally admired for its beauty, or which the owner sets particular store by, is termed a fancy article; as, a fancy clout, is a favourite handkerchief, etc.; so a woman who is the particular favourite of any man, is termed his fancy woman, and vice versa.

FAWNEY: a finger-ring.

FAWNIED, or FAWNEY-FAM'D: having one or more rings on the finger.

FEEDER: a spoon.

FENCE: a receiver of stolen goods; to fence any property, is to sell it to a receiver or other person.

FIB: a stick. To fib is to beat with a stick; also to box.

FIBBING-GLOAK, a pugilist.

FIBBING-MATCH: a boxing match.

FILE: a person who has had a long course of experience in the arts of fraud, so as to have become an adept, is termed an old file upon the

A New and Comprehensive Vocabulary of the Flash Language

town; so it is usual to say of a man who is extremely cunning, and not to be over-reached, that he is a deep file. File, in the old version of cant, signified a pickpocket, but the term is now obsolete.

FINGER-SMITH: a midwife.

FI'PENNY: a clasp-knife.

FLASH: the cant language used by the family. To speak good flash is to be well versed in cant terms.

FLASH: a person who affects any peculiar habit, as swearing, dressing in a particular manner, taking snuff, etc., merely to be taken notice of, is said to do it out of flash.

FLASH: to be flash to any matter or meaning, is to understand or comprehend it, and is synonymous with being fly, down, or awake; to put a person flash to any thing, is to put him on his guard, to explain or inform him of what he was before unacquainted with.

FLASH: to shew or expose any thing: as I flash'd him a bean, I shewed him a guinea. Don't flash your sticks, don't expose your pistols, etc.

FLASH-COVE, or COVESS: the landlord or landlady of a flash-ken.

FLASH-CRIB, FLASH-KEN, or FLASH-PANNY, a public-house resorted to chiefly by family people, the master of which is commonly an old prig, and not unfrequently an old-lag.

FLASH-MAN: a favourite or fancy-man; but this term is generally applied to those dissolute characters upon the town, who subsist upon the liberality of unfortunate women; and who, in return, are generally at hand during their nocturnal perambulations, to protect them should any brawl occur, or should they be detected in robbing those whom they have picked up.

FLASH-MOLLISHER: a family-woman.

FLASH-SONG: a song interlarded with flash words, generally relating to the exploits of the prigging fraternity in their various branches of depredation.

A New and Comprehensive Vocabulary of the Flash Language

FLESH-BAG: a shirt.

FLAT. In a general sense, any honest man, or square cove, in opposition to a sharp or cross-cove; when used particularly, it means the person whom you have a design to rob or defraud, who is termed the flat, or the flatty-gory. A man who does any foolish or imprudent act, is called a flat; any person who is found an easy dupe to the designs of the family, is said to be a prime flat. It's a good flat that's never down, is a proverb among flash people; meaning, that though a man may be repeatedly duped or taken in, he must in the end have his eyes opened to his folly.

FLAT-MOVE. Any attempt or project that miscarries, or any act of folly or mismanagement in human affairs is said to be a flat move.

FLATS: a cant name for playing-cards.

FLIP: to shoot.

FLOOR: to knock down anyone, either for the purpose of robbery, or to effect your escape, is termed flooring him.

FLOOR'D: a person who is so drunk, as to be incapable of standing, is said to be floor'd.

FLUE-FAKER: a chimney-sweeper.

FLY: vigilant; suspicious; cunning; not easily robbed or duped; a shopkeeper or person of this description, is called a fly cove, or a leary cove; on other occasions fly is synonymous with flash or leary, as, I'm fly to you, I was put flash to him, etc.

FLY THE MAGS: to gamble, by tossing up halfpence.

FOGLE: a silk handkerchief.

FORKS: the two forefingers of the hand; to put your forks down, is to pick a pocket.

FOSS, or PHOS: a phosphorus bottle used by cracksmen to obtain a light.

A New and Comprehensive Vocabulary of the Flash Language

FRISK: to search; to frisk a cly, is to empty a pocket of its contents; to stand frisk, is to stand search.

FRISK: fun or mirth of any kind.

GAFF: to gamble with cards, dice, etc., or to toss up.

GAFF: a country fair; also a meeting of gamblers for the purpose of play; any public place of amusement is liable to be called the gaff, when spoken of in flash company who know to what it alludes.

GALANEY: a fowl.

GALLOOT: a soldier.

GAME: every particular branch of depredation practised by the family, is called a game; as, what game do you go upon? One species of robbery or fraud is said to be a good game, another a queer game, etc.

GAMMON: flattery; deceit; pretence; plausible language; any assertion which is not strictly true, or professions believed to be insincere, as, I believe you're gammoning, or, that's all gammon, meaning, you are no doubt jesting with me, or, that's all a farce. To gammon a person, is to amuse him with false assurances, to praise, or flatter him, in order to obtain some particular end; to gammon a man to any act, is to persuade him to it by artful language, or pretence; to gammon a shop-keeper, etc., is to engage his attention to your discourse, while your accomplice is executing some preconcerted plan of depredation upon his property; a thief detected in a house which he has entered, upon the sneak, for the purpose of robbing it, will endeavour by some gammoning story to account for his intrusion, and to get off with a good grace; a man who is, ready at invention, and has always a flow of plausible language on these occasions, is said to be a prime gammoner; to gammon lushy or queer, is to pretend drunkenness, or sickness, for some private end.

GAMMON THE TWELVE: a man who has been tried by a criminal court, and by a plausible defence, has induced the jury to acquit him, or to banish the capital part of the charge, and so save his life, is said, by his associates to have gammoned the twelve in prime twig, alluding to the number of jurymen.

A New and Comprehensive Vocabulary of the Flash Language

GAMS: the legs, to have queer gams, is to be bandy-legged, or otherwise deformed.

GARNISH: a small sum of money extracted from a new chum on his entering a jail, by his fellow-prisoners, which affords them a treat of beer, gin, etc.

GARDEN: to put a person in the garden, in the hole, in the bucket, or in the well, are synonymous phrases, signifying to defraud him of his due share of the booty by embezzling a part of the property, or the money, it is fenced for; this phrase also applies generally to defrauding anyone with whom you are confidentially connected of what is justly his due.

GARRET: the fob-pocket.

GEORGY: a quartern-loaf.

GILL: a word used by way of variation, similar to cove, gloak, or gory; but generally coupled to some other descriptive term, as a flash-gill, a toby-gill, etc.

GIVE IT TO: to rob or defraud any place or person, as, I gave it to him for his reader, I robb'd him of his pocket-book. 'What suit did you give it them upon? In what manner, or by what means, did you effect your purpose? Also, to impose upon a person's credulity by telling him a string of falsehoods; or to take any unfair advantage of another's inadvertence or unsuspecting temper, on any occasion; in either case, the party at last dropping down, that is, detecting your imposition, will say, I believe you have been giving it to me nicely all this while.

GLAZE: a glass-window.

GLIM: a candle, or other light.

GLIM-STICK: a candlestick.

GLOAK: synonymous with GILL, which see.

GNARL: to gnarl upon a person, is the same as splitting or nosing upon him; a man guilty of this treachery is called a gnarling scoundrel, etc.

A New and Comprehensive Vocabulary of the Flash Language

GO-ALONGER: a simple easy person, who suffers himself to be made a tool of, and is readily persuaded to any act or undertaking by his associates, who inwardly laugh at his folly, and ridicule him behind his back.

GO OUT: to follow the profession of thieving; two or more persons who usually rob in company, are said to go out together.

GOOD: a place or person, which promises to be easily robbed, is said to be good, as, that house is good upon the crack; this shop is good upon the star; the swell is good for his montra; etc. A man who declares himself good for any favour or thing, means, that he has sufficient influence, or possesses the certain means to obtain it; good as bread, or good as cheese, are merely emphatical phrases to the same effect. See CAZ.

GORY: a term synonymous with cove, gill, or gloak, and like them, commonly used in the descriptive. See FLAT and SWELL.

GRAB: to seize; apprehend; take in custody; to make a grab at any thing, is to snatch suddenly, as at a gentleman's watch-chain, etc.

GRAB'D: taken, apprehended.

GRAY: a half-penny, or other coin, having two heads or two tails, and fabricated for the use of gamblers, who, by such a deception. frequently win large sums.

GROCERY: half-pence, or copper coin, in a collective sense.

GRUB: victuals of any kind; to grub a person, is to diet him, or find him in victuals; to grub well, is to eat with an appetite.

GUN: a view; look; observation; or taking notice; as, there is a strong gun at us, means, we are strictly observed. To gun any thing, is to look at or examine it.

HADDOCK: a purse; a haddock stuff'd with beans, is a jocular term for a purse full of guineas!

HALF A BEAN, HALF A QUID; half-a-guinea.

HALF A BULL: half-a-crown.

A New and Comprehensive Vocabulary of the Flash Language

HALF-FLASH AND HALF-FOOLISH: this character is applied sarcastically to a person, who has a smattering of the cant language, and having associated a little with family people, pretends to a knowledge of life which he really does not possess, and by this conduct becomes an object of ridicule among his acquaintance.

HAMMERISH: down as a hammer.

HANG IT ON: purposely to delay or protract the performance of any task or service you have undertaken, by dallying, and making as slow a progress as possible, either from natural indolence, or to answer some private end of your own, To hang it on with a woman, is to form a temporary connexion with her; to cohabit or keep company with her without marriage.

HANK: a bull-bait, or bullock-hunt.

HANK: to have a person at a good hank, is to have made any contract with him very advantageous to yourself; or to be able from some prior cause to command or use him just as you please; to have the benefit of his purse or other services, in fact, upon your own terms.

HANK: a spell of cessation from any work or duty, on the score of indisposition, or some other pretence.

HIGH-TOBY: the game of highway robbery, that is, exclusively on horseback.

HIGH-TOBY-GLOAK: a highwayman.

HIS-NABS: him or himself; a term used by way of emphasis, when speaking of a third person.

HOBBLED: taken up, or in custody; to hobble a plant, is to spring it. See PLANT.

HOG: a shilling; five, ten, or more shillings, are called five, ten, or more hog.

HOIST: the game of shop-lifting is called the hoist,. a person expert at this practice is said to be a goad hoist.

A New and Comprehensive Vocabulary of the Flash Language

HOLE. See GARDEN.

HOPPER-DOCKERS: shoes.

HORNEY: a constable.

HOXTER: an inside coat-pocket.

IN IT: to let another partake of any benefit or acquisition you have acquired by robbery or otherwise, is called putting him in it: a family-man who is accidentally witness to a robbery, etc., effected by one or more others, will say to the latter, Mind, I'm in it: which is generally acceded to, being the established custom; but there seems more of courtesy than right in this practice.

IN TOWN: flush of money; breeched.

JACOB: a ladder; a simple half-witted person.

JACK: a post-chaise.

JACK-BOY: a postillion.

JACKET: to jacket a person, or clap a jacket on him, is nearly synonymous with bridging him. See BRIDGE. But this term is more properly applied to removing a man by underhand and vile means from any birth or situation he enjoys, commonly with a view to supplant him; therefore, when a person, is supposed to have fallen a victim to such infamous machinations, it is said to have been a jacketing concern.

JASEY: a wig.

JEMMY, or JAMES: an iron-crow.

JERRY: a fog or mist.

JERVIS: a coachman.

JERVIS'S UPPER BENJAMIN: a box, or coachman's great coat.

JIGGER: a door.

A New and Comprehensive Vocabulary of the Flash Language

JOB: any concerted robbery, which is to be executed at a certain time, is spoken of by the parties as the job, or having a job to do at such a place; and in this case as regular preparations are made, and as great debates held, as about any legal business undertaken by the industrious part of the community.

JOGUE: a shilling; five jogue is five shillings, and so on, to any other number.

JOSKIN: a country-bumbkin.

JUDGE: a family-man, whose talents and experience have rendered him a complete adept in his profession, and who acts with a systematic prudence on all occasions, is allowed to be, and called by his friends, a fine judge.

JUDGEMENT: prudence; economy in acting; abilities, (the result of long experience,) for executing the most intricate and hazardous projects; any thing accomplished in a masterly manner, is, therefore, said to have been done with judgement; on concerting or planning any operations, one party will say, I think it would be judgement to do so and so, meaning expedient to do it.

JUDY: a blowen,. but sometimes used when speaking familiarly of any woman.

JUGELOW, a dog.

JUMP: a window on the ground-floor.

JUMP: a game, or species of robbery effected by getting into a house through any of the lower windows. To Jump a place, is to rob it upon the jump. A man convicted for this offence, is said to be done for a jump.

KELP: a hat; to kelp a person, is to move your hat to him.

KEMESA: a shirt.

KEN: a house; often joined to other descriptive terms, as, a flash ken, a bawdy-ken, etc.

KENT: a coloured pocket-handkerchief of cotton or linen.

A New and Comprehensive Vocabulary of the Flash Language

KICK: a sixpence, when speaking of compound sums only, as, three and a kick, is three and sixpence, etc.

KICKSEYS: breeches; speaking of a purse, etc., taken from the breeches pocket, they say, it was got from the kickseys, there being no cant term for the breeches pocket. To turn out a man's kickseys, means to pick the pockets of them, in which operation it is necessary to turn those pockets inside out, in order to get at the contents.

KID: a child of either sex, but particularly applied to a boy who commences thief at an early age; and when by his dexterity he has become famous, he is called by his acquaintances the kid so and so, mentioning his sirname.

KIDDY: a thief of the lower order, who, when he is breeched, by a course of successful depredation, dresses in the extreme of vulgar gentility, and affects a knowingness in his air and conversation, which renders him in reality an object of ridicule; such a one is pronounced by his associates of the same class, a flash-kiddy or a rolling-kiddy. My kiddy is a familiar term used by these gentry in addressing each other.

KID-RIG: meeting a child in the streets who is going on some errand, and by a false, but well fabricated story, obtaining any parcel or goods it may be carrying; this game is practised by two persons, who have each their respective parts to play, and even porters and other grown persons are sometimes defrauded of their load by this artifice. To kid a person out of any thing, is to obtain it from him by means of a false pretence, as that you were sent by a third person, etc. ; such impositions are all generally termed the kid-rig.

KINCHEN: a young lad.

KIRK: a church or chapel.

KNAP: to steal; take; receive; accept; according to the sense it is used in; as, to knap a clout, is to steal a pocket-handkerchief; to knap the swag from your pall, is to take from him the property he has just stolen, for the purpose of carrying it; to knap seven or fourteen pen'worth, is to receive sentence of transportation for seven or fourteen years; to knap the glim, is to catch the venereal disease; in making a bargain, to knap the sum offered you, is to accept it;

A New and Comprehensive Vocabulary of the Flash Language

speaking of a woman supposed to be pregnant, it is common to say, I believe Mr. Knap is concerned, meaning that she has knap'd.

KNAPPING A JACOB FROM A DANNA-DRAG: This is a curious species of robbery, or rather borrowing without leave, for the purpose of robbery; it signifies taking away the short ladder from a nightman's cart, while the men are gone into a house, the privy of which they are employed emptying, in order to effect an ascent to a one-pair-of-stairs window, to scale a garden-wall, etc., after which the ladder, of course, is left to rejoin its master as it can.

KNIFE IT. See CHEESE IT.

KNUCK, KNUCKLER, or KNUCKLING-COVE: a pickpocket, or person professed in the knuckling art.

KNUCKLE: to pick pockets, but chiefly applied to the more refined branch of that art, namely, extracting notes, loose cash, etc., from the waistcoat or breeches pockets, whereas buzzing is used in a more general sense. See BUZ.

LAG: to transport for seven years or upwards.

LAG: a convict under sentence of transportation.

LAG: to make water. To lag spirits, wine, etc., is to adulterate them with water.

LAGGER: a sailor.

LAGGING-DUES: speaking of a person likely to be transported, they say lagging dues will be concerned.

LAGGING MATTER: any species of crime for which a person is liable on conviction to be transported.

LAG SHIP: a transport chartered by Government for the conveyance of convicts to New South Wales; also, a hulk, or floating prison, in which, to the disgrace of humanity, many hundreds of these unhappy persons are confined, and suffer every complication of human misery.

LAMPS: the eyes; to have queer lamps, is to have sore or weak eyes.

A New and Comprehensive Vocabulary of the Flash Language

LARK: fun or sport of any kind, to create which is termed knocking up a lark.

LAWN: a white cambric handkerchief.

LEARY: synonymous with fly.

LEARY-COVE. See FLY.

LEATHER-LANE: any thing paltry, or of a bad quality, is called a Leather-lane concern.

LETTER Q: the mace, or billiard-slum, is sometimes called going upon the Q, or the letter Q, alluding to an instrument used in playing billiards.

LETTER-RACKET: going about to respectable houses with a letter or statement, detailing some case of extreme distress, as shipwreck, sufferings by fire, etc. ; by which many benevolent, but credulous, persons, are induced to relieve the fictitious wants of the imposters, who are generally men, or women, of genteel address, and unfold a plausible tale of affliction.

LEVANTING, or RUNNING A LEVANT: an expedient practised by broken gamesters to retrieve thcmselves, and signifies to bet money at a race, cockmatch, etc., without a shilling in their pocket to answer the event. The punishment for this conduct in a public cockpit is rather curious; the offender is placed in a large basket, kept on purpose, which is then hoisted up to the ceiling or roof of the building, and the party is there kept suspended, and exposed to derision during the pleasure of the company.

LIFE: by this term is meant the various cheats and deceptions practised by the designing part of mankind; a person well versed in this kind of knowledge, is said to be one that knows life; in other words, that knows the world. This is what Goldsmith defines to be a knowledge of human nature on the wrong side.

LIGHT: to inform of any robbery, etc., which has been some time executed and concealed, is termed bringing the affair to light,. to produce any thing to view, or to give up any stolen property for the sake of a reward, to quash a prosecution, is also called bringing it to

A New and Comprehensive Vocabulary of the Flash Language

light. A thief, urging his associates to a division of any booty they have lately made, will desire them to bring the swag to light.

LILL: a pocket-book.

LINE: to get a person in a line, or in a string, is to engage them in a conversation, while your confederate is robbing their person or premises; to banter or jest with a man by amusing him with false assurances or professions, is also termed stringing him, or getting him in tow; to keep any body in suspense on any subject without coming to a decision, is called keeping him in tow, in a string, or in a tow-line. To cut the line, or the string, is to put an end to the suspense in which you have kept anyone, by telling him the plain truth, coming to a final decision, etc. A person, who has been telling another a long story, until he is tired, or conceives his auditor has been all the while secretly laughing at him, will say at last, I've just dropped down, you've had me in a fine string, I think it's time to cut it. On the other hand, the auditor, having the same opinion on his part, would say, Come, I believe you want to string me all night, I wish you'd cut it; meaning, conclude the story at once.

LOB: a till, or money-drawer. To have made a good lob, is synonymous with making a good speak.

LOCK-UP-CHOVEY: a covered cart, in which travelling hawkers convey their goods about the country; and which is secured by a door, lock, and key.

LODGING-SLUM: the practice of hiring ready furnished lodgings, and stripping them of the plate, linen, and other valuables.

LOOK AT A PLACE: when a plan is laid for robbing a house, etc., upon the crack, or the screw, the parties will go a short time before the execution, to examine the premises, and make any necessary observations; this is called looking at the place.

LOUR: money.

LUMBER: a room.

LUMBER: to lumber any property, is to deposit it at a pawnbroker's, or elsewhere for present security; to retire to any house or private place, for a short time, is called lumbering yourself. A man

A New and Comprehensive Vocabulary of the Flash Language

apprehended, and sent to gaol, is said to be lumbered, to be in lumber, or to be in Lombard-street.

LUSH: to drink; speaking of a person who is drunk, they say, Alderman Lushington is concerned, or, he has been voting for the Alderman.

LUSH: beer or liquor of any kind.

LUSH-CRIB, or LUSH-KEN: a public-house, or gin-shop.

LUSH, or LUSHY, drunk, intoxicated.

LUSHY-COVE: a drunken man.

MACE: to mace a shopkeeper, or give it to him upon the mate, is to obtain goods on credit, which you never mean to pay for; to run up a score with the same intention, or to spunge upon your acquaintance, by continually begging or borrowing from them, is termed maceing, or striking the mace.

MACE-GLOAK: a man who lives upon the mace.

MAG: a halfpenny.

MANCHESTER: the tongue.

MANG: to speak or talk.

MAULEY: the hand.

MAX: gin or hollands.

MILESTONE: a country booby.

MILL: to fight. To mill a 'person is to beat him.

MILL A GLAZE: to break a window.

MILL-DOLL: an obsolete name for Bridewell house of correction, in Bridge-street, Blackfriars, London.

MILLING-COVE: a pugilist.

A New and Comprehensive Vocabulary of the Flash Language

MITTS: gloves.

MITTENS: the hands.

MIZZLE: to quit or go away from any place or company; to elope, or run away.

MOLLISHER: a woman.

MONKEY: a padlock.

MONKERY: the country parts of England are called The Monkery.

MANTRA: a watch.

MORNING-SNEAK: going out early to rob private houses or shops by slipping in at the door unperceived, while the servant or shopman is employed in cleaning the steps, windows, etc.

MOTT: a blowen, or woman of the town.

MOUNT: to swear, or give evidence falsely for the sake of a gratuity. To mount for a person is also synonymous with bonnetting for him.

MOUNTER: a man who lives by mounting, or perjury, who is always ready for a guinea or two to swear whatever is proposed to him.

MOUTH: a foolish silly person; a man who does a very imprudent act, is said to be a rank mouth.

MOVE: any action or operation in life; the secret spring by which any project is conducted, as, There is a move in that business which you are not down to. To be flash to every move upon the board, is to have a general knowledge of the world, and all its numerous deceptions.

MR. KNAP. See KNAP.

MR. NASH. See NASH.

MR. PALMER. See PALM.

A New and Comprehensive Vocabulary of the Flash Language

MR. PULLEN. See PULL or PULL UP.

MUFF: an epithet synonymous with mouth.

MUG: the face; a queer mug is an ugly face.

MURPHY'S COUNTENANCE: a pig's face.

MYNABS: me, myself.

NAIL: to nail a person, is to over-reach, or take advantage of him in the course of trade or traffic; also, to rob, or steal; as, I nail'd him for (or of) his reader, I robbed him of his pocket-book; I nail'd the swell's mantra in the push, I picked the gentleman's pocket of his watch in the crowd, etc. A person of an over-reaching, imposing disposition, is called a nail, a dead nail, a nailing rascal, a rank needle, or a needle pointer.

NANCY: the posteriors.

NAP the BIB: to cry; as, the mollisher nap'd her bib, the woman fell a crying.

NASH: to go away from, or quit, any place or company; speaking of a person who is gone, they say, he is nash'd, or Mr. Nash is concerned.

NE-DASH: nothing.

NEEDLE: (see NAIL) to needle a person is to haggle with him in making a bargain, and, if possible, take advantage of him, though in the most trifling article.

NEEDLE-POINTER. See NAIL.

NEEDY-MIZZLER: a poor ragged object of either sex; a shabby-looking person.

NIB: a gentleman, or person of the higher order. People who affect gentility or consequence, without any real pretensions thereto, arc from hence vulgarly called Half-nibs or Half-swells; and, indeed, persons of low minds, who conceive money to be the only criterion of gentility, arc too apt to stigmatize with the before-mentioned

A New and Comprehensive Vocabulary of the Flash Language

epithets any man, 'who, however well-bred and educated, may be reduced to a shabby external, but still preserves a sense of decorum in his manners, and avoids associating with the vagabonds among whom he may unfortunately be doomed to exist.

NIBB'D: taken in custody.

NIBBLE: to pilfer trifling articles, not having spirit to touch any thing of consequence.

NIBBLER: a pilferer or petty thief.

NIX, or NIX MY DOLL: nothing.

NOB IT: to act with such prudence and knowledge of the world, as to prosper and become independent without any labour or bodily exertion; this is termed nobbing it, or fighting nob work. To effect any purpose, or obtain any thing, by means of good judgment and sagacity, is called nabbing it for such a thing.

NOB-PITCHERS: a general term for those sharpers who attend at fairs, races, etc., to take in the flats at prick in the garter, cups and balls, and other similar artifices.

NO DOWN. See FAKE AWAY, etc.

NOSE: a thief who becomes an evidence against his accomplices; also, a person who seeing one or more suspicious characters in the streets, makes a point of watching them in order to frustrate any attempt they may make, or to cause their apprehension; also, a spy or informer of any description.

NOSE: to nose, is to pry into any person's proceedings in an impertinent manner. To nose upon anyone, is to tell of any thing he has said or done with a view to injure him, or to benefit yourself.

NULLING-COVE: a pugilist.

NUT: to please a person by any little act of assiduity, by a present, or by flattering words, is called nutting him; as the present, etc., by 'which you have gratified them, is termed a nut.

A New and Comprehensive Vocabulary of the Flash Language

NUTS UPON IT: to be very much pleased or gratified with any object, adventure, or overture; so a person who conceives a strong inclination for another of the opposite sex, is said to be quite nutty, or nuts upon him or her.

NUTS UPON YOURSELF: a man who is much gratified with any bargain he has made, narrow escape he has had, or other event in which he is interested, will express his self-satisfaction or gladness by declaring that he is, or was, quite nuts upon himself.

OFFICE: a hint, signal, or private intimation, from one person to another; this is termed officeing him, or giving him the office; to take the office, is to understand and profit by the hint given.

OLD LAG: a man or woman who has been transported, is so called on returning home, by those who are acquainted with the secret. See LAG.

OLIVER: the moon.

OLIVER IS IN TOWN: a phrase signifying that the nights are moonlight, and consequently unfavourable to depredation.

OLIVER'S UP: the moon has risen.

OLIVER WHIDDLES: the moon shines.

ONE UPON YOUR TAW: a person who takes offence at the conduct of another, or conceives himself injured by the latter, will say, never mind, I'll be one upon your taw; or, I'll be a marble on your taw; meaning, I'll be even with you some time.

ONION: a watch-seal, a bunch if onions, is several seals worn upon one ring.

ORDER-RACKET: obtaining goods from a shopkeeper, by means of a forged order or false pretence.

OUT-AND-OUT: quite; completely; effectually. See SERVE and FAKE.

OUT-AND-OUTER: a person of a resolute determined spirit, who pursues his object without regard to danger or difficulties; also an

A New and Comprehensive Vocabulary of the Flash Language

incorrigible depredator, who will rob friend or stranger indiscriminately, being possessed of neither honour nor principle.

OUT OF FLASH. See FLASH.

OUT OF THE WAY: a thief who knows that he is sought after by the traps on some information, and consequently goes out of town, or otherwise conceals himself, is said by his palls to be out if the way for so and so, naming the particular offence he stands charged with. See WANTED.

OUT OF TWIG, to put yourself out of twig, is to disguise your dress and appearance, to avoid being recognised, on some particular account; a man reduced by poverty to wear a shabby dress is said by his acquaintance to be out if twig; to put any article out of twig, as a stolen coat, cloak, etc., is to alter it in such a way that it cannot be identified.

PALL: a partner; companion; associate; or accomplice.

PALM: to bribe, or give money, for the attainment of any object or indulgence; and it is then said that the party who receives it is palmed, or that Mr. Palmer is concerned.

PALMING-RACKET: secreting money in the palm of the hand, a game at which some are very expert.

PANNY: a house.

PANNUM: bread.

PARK. See BUSHY-PARK.

PATTER: to talk; as, He patters good flash, etc.

PATTER'D: tried in a court of justice; a man who has undergone this ordeal, is said to have stood the patter.

PEAR-MAKING: inlisting in various regiments, taking the bounty, and then deserting.

A New and Comprehensive Vocabulary of the Flash Language

PENSIONER: a mean-spirited fellow who lives with a woman of the town, and suffers her to maintain him in idleness in the character of her fancy-man.

PETER: a parcel or bundle, whether large or small; but most properly it signifies a trunk or box.

PETER-HUNTING: traversing the streets or roads for the purpose of cutting away trunks, etc., from travelling carriages; persons who follow this game, are from thence called peter-hunters, whereas the drag more properly applies to robbing carts or wagons.

PETER-HUNTING-JEMMY: a small iron crow, particularly adapted for breaking the patent chain, with which the luggage is of late years secured to gentlemen's carriages; and which, being of steel, case-hardened, is fallaciously supposed to be proof against the attempts of thieves.

PETER-THAT: synonymous with Stow-that.

PICK-UP: to accost, or enter into conversation with any person, for the purpose of executing some design upon his personal property; thus, among gamblers, it is called Picking up a flat, or a mouth: sharpers, who are daily on the look-out for some unwary countryman or stranger, use the same phrase; and among drop-coves, and others who act in concert, this task is allotted to one of the gang, duly qualified, who is thence termed the picker-up; and he having performed his part, his associates proceed systematically in cleaning out the flat. To pick up a cull, is a term used by blowens in their vocation of street-walking. To pick a person up, in a general sense, is to impose upon, or take advantage of him, in a contract or bargain.

PIGS, or GRUNTERS: police runners.

PINS: the legs.

PINCH: to purloin small articles of value in the shops of jewellers, etc., while pretending to purchase or bespeak some trinket. This game is called the Pinch—I pinch'd him for a fawney, signifies I purloined a ring from him; Did you pinch any thing ill that crib? did you succeed ill secreting any thing in that shop? This game is a branch of shoplifting; but when the hoist is spoken of, it commonly

A New and Comprehensive Vocabulary of the Flash Language

applies to stealing articles of a larger, though less valuable, kind, as pieces of muslin, or silk handkerchiefs, printed cotton, etc. See HOIST.

PINCH-GLOAK: a man who works upon the pinch.

PIPES: boots.

PIT: the bosom pocket in a coat.

PIT-MAN: a pocket-book worn in the bosom-pocket.

PITCHER. Newgate in London is called by various names, as the pitcher, the stone Pitcher, the start, and the stone jug, according to the humour of the speaker.

PLANT. To hide, or conceal any person or thing, is termed Planting him, or it; and any thing hid is called, the plant, when alluded to in conversation; such article is said to be in plant; the place of concealment is sometimes called the plant, as, I know of a fine plant; that is, a secure hiding-place. To spring a plant, is to find any thing that has been concealed by another. To rise the plant, is to take up and remove any thing that has been hid, whether by yourself or another. A person's money, or valuables, secreted about his house, or person, is called his plant. To plant upon a man, is to set somebody to watch his motions; also to place any thing purposely in his way, that he may steal it and be immediately detected.

PLAY A-CROSS. What is commonly termed playing booty, that is, purposely losing the game, or match, in order to take in the flats who have backed you, (see BRIDGE) while the sharps divide the spoil, in which you have a share. This sort of treachery extends to boxing, racing, and every other species of sport, on which bets are laid; sometimes a sham match is made for the purpose of inducing strangers to bet, which is decided in such a manner that the latter will inevitably lose. A-cross signifies generally any collusion or unfair dealing between several parties.

PLUMMY. Right; very good; as it should be; expressing your approbation of any act, or event, you will say, That's plummy, or It's all plummy; meaning it is all right.

POGUE. A bag, (probably a corruption of poke.)

A New and Comprehensive Vocabulary of the Flash Language

POPS. Pistols; an obsolete term.

POST, or POST THE PONEY. To stake, or lay down the money, as on laying a bet, or concluding a bargain.

POUNDABLE. Any event which is considered certain or inevitable, is declared to be poundable, as the issue of a game, the success of a bet, etc.

POUND IT. To ensure or make a certainty of any thing; thus, a man will say, I'll pound it to be so; taken, probably from the custom of laying, or rather offering ten pounds to a crown at a cock-match, in which case, if no person takes this extravagant odds, the battle is at an end. This is termed pounding a cock.

PRAD. A horse.

PRADBACK. Horseback.

PRIG. A thief.

PRIG. To steal; to go out a-prigging, is to go a-thieving.

PRIME. In a general sense, synonymous with plummy; any thing very good of its kind, is called a prime article. Any thing executed in a stylish or masterly manner, is said to be done in prime twig. See FAKEMENT, and GAMMON THE TWELVE.

PULL. An important advantage possessed by one party over another; as in gaming, you may by some slight, unknown to your adversary, or by a knowledge of the cards, etc., have the odds of winning considerably on your side; you are then said to have a great pull. To have the power of injuring a person, by the knowledge of any thing erroneous in his conduct, which leaves his character or personal safety at your mercy, is also termed having a pull upon him, that is (to use a vulgar phrase) that you have him under your thumb. A person speaking of any intricate affair, or feat of ingenuity, which he cannot comprehend, will say, There is some pull at the bottom of it, that I'm not fly to.

PULL, or PULL UP: to accost; stop; apprehend; or take into custody; as to pull up a Jack, is to stop a post-chaise on the highway. To pull a

A New and Comprehensive Vocabulary of the Flash Language

man, or have him pulled, is to cause his apprehension for some offence; and it is then said, that Mr. Pullen is concerned.

PULLED, PULLED UP, or IN PULL: Taken in custody; in confinement.

PUSH: a crowd or concourse of people, either in the streets, or at any public place of amusement, etc., when any particular scene of crowding is alluded to, they say, the push, as the push, at the spell doors; the push at the stooping-match, etc.

PUT DOWN. See DOWN.

PUT FLASH. See FLASH.

PUT FLY. See FLY.

PUT UP: to suggest to another, the means of committing a depredation, or effecting any other business, is termed, putting him up to it.

PUT UP AFFAIR: any preconcerted plan or scheme to effect a robbery, etc., undertaken at the suggestion of another person, who possessing a knowledge of the premises, is competent to advise the principal how best to proceed.

PUTTER UP: the projector or planner of a put-up affair, as a servant in a gentleman's family, who proposes to a gang of housebreakers the robbery of his master's house, and informs them where the plate, etc., is deposited, (instances of which are frequent in London) is termed the putter up, and usually shares equally in the booty with the parties executing, although the former may lie dormant, and take no part in the actual commission of the fact.

PUZZLING-STICKS: the triangles to which culprits are tied up, for the purpose of undergoing flagellation.

Q. See LETTER Q.

QUEER: bad; counterfeit; false; unwell in health.

QUEER, or QUEER-BIT: base money.

A New and Comprehensive Vocabulary of the Flash Language

QUEER SCREENS: forged Bank-notes.

QUEER IT: to spoil it, which see.

QUEER-BAIL. Persons of no repute, hired to bail a prisoner in any bailable case; these men are to be had in London for a trifling sum, and are called Broomsticks.

QUID: a guinea.

QUOD: a gaol. To quod a person is to send him to gaol. In quod, is in gaol.

QUOD-COVE: the keeper of a gaol.

QUODDING-DUES. See DUES.

RACKET: some particular kinds of fraud and robbery are so termed, when called by their flash titles, and others Rig; as, the Letter-racket, the Order-racket; the Kid-rig; the Cat and Kitten-rig, etc., but all these terms depend upon the fancy of the speaker. In fact, any game may be termed a rig, racket, suit, slum, etc., by prefixing thereto the particular branch of depredation or fraud in question, many examples of which occur in this work.

RAG: money.

RAG-GORGY: a rich or monied man, but generally used in conversation when a particular gentleman, or person high in office, is hinted at; instead of mentioning his name, they say, the Rag-gorgy, knowing themselves to be understood by those they are addressing. See COVE, and SWELL.

RAMP: to rob any person or place by open violence or suddenly snatching at something and running off with it, as, I ramp'd him of his montra; why did you not ramp his castor? etc. A man convicted of this offence, is said to have been done for a ramp. This audacious game, is called by prigs, the ramp, and is nearly similar to the RUSH, which see.

RANK: complete; absolute, downright, an emphatical manner of describing persons or characters, as a rank nose, a rank swell, etc. etc.

A New and Comprehensive Vocabulary of the Flash Language

RATTLER: a coach.

READER: a pocket-book.

READER-HUNTERS. See DUMMY-HUNTERS.

REGULARS: one's due share of a booty, etc. on a division taking place. Give me my regulars, that is, give me my dividend.

REIGN: the length or continuance of a man's career in a system of wickedness, which when he is ultimately bowled out, is said to have been a long, or a short reign, according to its duration.

RESURRECTION-COVE: a stealer of dead bodies.

RIBBAND: money in general.

RIDGE: gold, whether in coin or any other shape, as a ridge montra, a gold watch; a cly-full of ridge, a pocket full of gold.

RIG. See RACKET.

RINGING, or RINGING-IN: to ring is to exchange; ringing the changes, is a fraud practised by smashers, who when they receive good money in change of a guinea, etc., ring-in one or more pieces of base with great dexterity, and then request the party to change them.

RINGING CASTORS: signifies frequenting churches and other public assemblies, for the purpose of changing hats, by taking away a good, and leaving a shabby one in its place; a petty game now seldom practised.

RISE THE PLANT. See PLANT.

ROCK'D: superannuated, forgetful, absent in mind; old lags are commonly said to be thus affected, probably caused by the sufferings they have undergone.

ROLLERS: horse and foot patrole, who parade the roads round about London during the night, for the prevention of robberies.

ROMANY: a gypsy; to patter romany, is to talk the gypsy flash.

A New and Comprehensive Vocabulary of the Flash Language

ROOK: a small iron crow.

ROUGH-FAM, or ROUGH-FAMMY: the waistcoat pocket.

ROW IN THE BOAT: to go snacks, or have a share in the benefit arising from any transaction to which you are privy. To let a person row with you, is to admit him to a share.

RUFFLES. Handcuffs.

RUGGINS'S: to go to bed, is called going to Ruggins's.

RUM: good, in opposition to queer.

RUMBLE-TUMBLE: a stage-coach.

RUMP'D: flogged or scourged.

RUMPUS: a masquerade.

RUSH: the rush, is nearly synonymous with the ramp; but the latter often applies to snatching at a single article, as a silk cloak, for instance, from a milliner's shop-door; whereas a rush may signify a forcible entry by several men into a detached dwelling-house for the purpose of robbing its owners of their money, etc. A sudden and violent effort to get into any place, or vice-versa to effect your exit, as from a place of confinement, etc., is called rushing them, or giving it to 'em upon the rush.

RUSSIAN COFFEE-HOUSE: a name given by some punster of the family, to the Brown Bear public-house in Bow-street, Covent-garden.

SACK: a pocket; to sack any thing is to pocket it.

SALT-BOXES: the condemned cells in Newgate are so called.

SALT-BOX-CLY: the outside coat-pocket, with a flap.

SAND: moist sugar.

SAWNEY: bacon.

A New and Comprehensive Vocabulary of the Flash Language

SCAMP: the game of highway robbery is called the scamp. To scamp a person is to rob him on the highway. Done for a scamp signifies convicted of a highway robbery.

SCAMP, or SCAMPSMAN: a highwayman.

SCHOOL: a party of persons met together for the purpose of gambling.

SCOT: a person of an irritable temper, who is easily put in a passion, which is often done by the company he is with, to create fun; such a one is declared to be a fine scot. This diversion is called getting him out, or getting him round the corner, from these terms being used by bull-hankers, with whom also a scot is a bullock of a particular breed, which affords superior diversion when hunted.

SCOTTISH: fiery, irritable, easily provoked.

SCOUT: a watchman.

SCOUT-KEN: a watch-house.

SCRAG'D: hang'd.

SCRAGGING-POST: the gallows.

SCREEN: a bank-note.

SCREEVE: a letter, or writing paper.

SCREW: a skeleton or false key. To screw a place is to enter it by false keys; this game is called the screw. Any robbery effected by such means is termed a screw.

SCREWSMAN: a thief who goes out a screwing.

SCURF'D: taken in custody.

SEEDY: poor, ragged in appearance, shabby.

SELL: to sell a man is to betray him, by giving information against him, or otherwise to injure him clandestinely for the sake of interest, nearly the same as bridgeing him. (See BRIDGE.) A man who falls a victim to any treachery of this kind, is said to have been sold like a bullock in Smithfield.

SERVE: to serve a person, or place, is to rob them; as, I serv'd him for his thimble, I rob'd him of his watch; that crib has been served before, that shop has been already robbed, etc. To serve a man, also sometimes signifies to maim, wound, or do him some bodily hurt; and to serve him out and out, is to kill him.

SHAKE: to steal, or rob; as, I shook a chest of slop, I stole a chest of tea; I've been shook of my skin, I have been robbed of my purse. A thief, whose pall has been into any place for the purpose of robbery, will say on his coming out, Well, is it all right, have you shook? meaning, did you succeed in getting any thing? When two persons rob in company, it is generally the province, or part, of one to shake, (that is, obtain the swagg), and the other to carry, (that is, bear it to a place of safety).

SHALLOW: a hat.

SHAN: counterfeit money in general.

SHARP: a gambler, or person, professed in all the arts of play; a cheat, or swindler; any cross-cove, in general, is called a sharp, in opposition to a flat, or square-cove; but this is only in a comparative sense in the course of conversation.

SHARPING: swindling and cheating in all their various forms, including the arts of fraud at play.

SHIFTER: an alarm, or intimation, given by a thief to his pall, signifying that there is a down, or that some one is approaching, and that he had, therefore, better desist from what he is about.

SHINER: a looking-glass.

SHOOK: synonymous with rock'd.

SHOVE-UP: nothing.

SHUTTER-RACKET: the practice of robbing houses, or shops, by boring a hole in the window shutter, and taking out a pane of glass.

A New and Comprehensive Vocabulary of the Flash Language

SINGLE-HANDED: robbery by yourself, without a pall.

SIR SYDNEY: a clasp knife.

SKIN. a purse, or money bag.

SKIN: to strip a man of all his money at play, is termed skinning him.

SLANG. A watch chain, a chain of any kind; also a warrant, license to travel, or other official instrument.

SLANG: to defraud a person of any part of his due, is called slanging him; also to cheat by false weights or measures, or other unfair means.

SLANG WEIGHTS, or MEASURES: unjust, or defective ones.

SLANGING-DUES: 'when a man suspects that he has been curtailed, or cheated, of any portion of his just right, he will say, there has been slanging-dues concerned.

SLANG'D: fettered.

SLANGS: fetters, or chains of any kind used about prisoners; body-slangs are body-irons used on some occasions.

SLAVEY: a servant of either sex.

SLIP: the slash pocket in the skirt of a coat behind.

SLOP: tea.

SLOP-FEEDER: a tea-spoon.

SLOUR: to lock, secure, or fasten; to slour up is also to button up; as one's coat, pocket, etc.

SLOUR'D, or SLOUR'D UP: locked, fastened, buttoned, etc.

SLUM: a room.

SLUM. See RACKET and LODGING-SLUM.

SLY. Any business transacted, or intimation given, privately, or under the rose, is said to be done upon the sly.

SMASHER: a man or woman who follows the game of smashing.

SMASHING: uttering counterfeit money; smashing of queer screens, signifies uttering forged bank notes. To smash a guinea, note, or other money, is, in a common sense, to procure, or give, change for it.

SMISH: a shirt.

SMUT: a copper boiler, or furance.

SNEAK: The sneak is the practice of robbing houses or shops, by slipping in unperceived, and taking whatever may lay most convenient; this is commonly the first branch of thieving, in which young boys are initiated, who, from their size and activity, appear well adapted for it. To sneak a place, is to rob it upon the sneak. A sneak is a robbery effected in the above manner. One or more prisoners having escaped from their confinement by stealth, without using any violence, or alarming their keepers, arc said to have sneak'd 'em, or given it to 'em upon the sneak. See RUSH.

SNEAKSMAN: a man or boy who goes upon the sneak.

SNEEZER, or SNEEZING-COFER: a snuff-box.

SNITCH: to impeach, or betray your accomplices, is termed snitching upon them. A person who becomes king's evidence on such an occasion, is said to have turned snitch; an informer, or talebearer, in general, is called a snitch, or a snitching rascal, in which sense snitching is synonymous with nosing, or coming it.

SNIPES: scissors.

SNIV: an expression synonymous with bender, and used in the same manner.

SNOW: clean linen from the washerwoman's hands, whether it be wet or dry, is termed snow.

A New and Comprehensive Vocabulary of the Flash Language

SNOOZE: to sleep; a snooze sometimes means a lodging; as, Where can I get a snooze for this darky instead of saying a bed.

SNUFFING: going into a shop on some pretence, watching an opportunity to throw a handful of snuff in the eyes of the shopkeeper, and then running off with any valuable article you can lay hands on; this is called snuffing him, or giving it to him upon the snuff racket.

SOLD. See SELL.

SOUND: to sound a person, means generally to draw from him, in an artful manner, any particulars you want to be acquainted with; as, to sound a kid, porter, etc., is to pump out of him the purport of his errand, the contents of his bundle, or load, etc., that your pall may know how to accost him, in order to draw the swag. See DRAW and KID-RIG. To sound a cly, is to touch a person's pocket gently on the outside, in order to ascertain the nature of its contents.

SPANGLE: a seven-shilling piece.

SPANK: to spank a glaze, is to break a pane of glass in a shop window, and make a sudden snatch at some article of value within your reach, having previously tied the shop-door with a strong cord on the outside, so as to prevent the shopman from getting out, till you have had full time to escape with your booty; to spank a place, is to rob it upon the spank, a spank is a robbery effected by the above means.

SPEAK: committing any robbery; is called making a speak; and if it has been productive, you are said to have made a rum speak.

SPEAK TO: to speak to a person or place is to rob them, and to speak to any article, is to steal it; as, I spoke to the cove for his montra; I robb'd the gentleman of his watch. I spoke to that crib for all the wedge; I robb'd that house of all the plate. I spoke to a chest of slop; I stole a chest of tea. A thief will say to his pall who has been attempting any robbery, "Well, did you speak? or, have you spoke? " meaning, did you get any thing?

SPELL: the play-house.

A New and Comprehensive Vocabulary of the Flash Language

SPICE: the spice is the game of footpad robbery; describing an exploit of this nature; a rogue will say, I spiced a swell of so much, naming the booty obtained. A spice is a footpad robbery.

SPICE GLOAK: a footpad robber.

SPIN A YARN. See YARN.

SPLIT: to split upon a person, or turn split, is synonymous with nosing, snitching, or turning nose. To split signifies generally to tell of any thing you hear, or see transacted.

SPOIL IT: to throw some obstacle in the way of any project or undertaking, so as to cause its failure, is termed spoiling it. In like manner, to prevent another person from succeeding in his object, either by a wilful obstruction, or by some act of imprudence on your part, subjects you to the charge of having spoiled him. Speaking of some particular species of fraud or robbery, which after a long series of success, is now become stale or impracticable from the public being guarded against it, the family will say, that game is spoiled at last. So having attempted the robbery of any particular house or shop, and by miscarrying caused such an alarm as to render a second attempt dangerous or impolitic, they will say, that place is spoil'd, it is useless to try it on any more.

SPOKE TO: alluding to any person or place that has been already robbed, they say, that place, or person, has been spoke to before. A family man on discovering that he has been robbed, will exclaim, I have been spoke to, and perhaps will add, for such a thing, naming what he has lost. Spoke to upon the screw, crack, sneak, hoist, buz, etc. etc., means robbed upon either of those particular suits or games. Upon any great misfortune befalling a man, as being apprehended on a very serious charge, receiving a wound supposed to be mortal, etc., his friends will say, Poor fellow, I believe he's spoke to, meaning it is all over with him.

SPOONY: foolish, half-witted, nonsensical; a man who has been drinking till he becomes disgusting by his very ridiculous behaviour, is said to be spoony drunk; and, from hence it is usual to call a very prating shallow fellow, a rank spoon.

SPOUT: to pledge any property at a pawnbroker's is termed spouting it, or shoving it up the spout.

A New and Comprehensive Vocabulary of the Flash Language

SPREAD: butter.

SPRING THE PLANT. See PLANT.

SQUARE: all fair, upright, and honest practices, are called the square, in opposition to the cross. Any thing you have bought, or acquired honestly, is termed a square article,. and any transaction which is fairly and equitably conducted, is said to be a square concern. A tradesman or other person who is considered by the world to be an honest man, and who is unacquainted with family people, and their system of operations, is by the latter emphatically styled a square cove, whereas an old thief who has acquired an independence, and now confines himself to square practices, is still called by his old palls a flash cove, who has tyed up prigging. See GROSS and FLAT. In making a bargain or contract, any overture considered to be really fair and reasonable, is declared to be a square thing, or to be upon the square. To be upon the square with any person, is to have mutually settled all accompts between you both up to that moment. To threaten another that you will be upon the square with him, some time, signifies that you'll be even with him for some supposed injury, etc.

SQUARE-COVE. See SQUARE.

SQUARE-CRIB: a respectable house, of good repute, whose inmates, their mode of life and connexions, are all perfectly on the square. See CROSS-CRIB.

SQUEEZE: the neck.

STAG: to turn stag was formerly synonymous with turning nose, or snitching, but the phrase is now exploded.

STAG: to stag any object or person, is to look at, observe, or take notice of them.

STAINES: a man who is in pecuniary distress is said to be at Staines, or at the Bush, alluding to the Bush inn at that town. See BUSH'D.

STAKE: a booty acquired by robbery, or a sum of money won at play, is called a stake, and if considerable, a prime stake, or a heavy stake. A person alluding to any thing difficult to be procured, or which he obtains as a great favour, and is therefore comparatively

A New and Comprehensive Vocabulary of the Flash Language

invaluable, would say, I consider it a stake to get it at all; a valuable or acceptable acquisition of any kind, is emphatically called a stake, meaning a great prize.

STALL: a violent pressure in a crowd, made by pick-pockets for the more easily effecting their depredatory purposes; this is called making a rum stall in the push.

STALL OFF: a term variously applied; generally it means a pretence, excuse, or prevarication-as a person charged 'with any fault, entering into some plausible story, to excuse himself, his hearers or accusers would say, O yes, that's a good stall off, or, Aye, aye, stall it off that way if you can. To extricate a person from any dilemma, or save him from disgrace, is called stalling him off; as an accomplice of your's being detected in a robbery, etc., and about to be given up to justice, you will step up as a stranger, interfere in his behalf, and either by vouching for his innocence, recommending lenity, or some other artifice, persuade his accusers to forego their intention, and let the prisoner escape; you will then boast of having stalled him off in prime twig. To avoid or escape any impending evil or punishment by means of artifice, submission, bribe, or otherwise, is also called stalling it off. A man walking the streets, and passing a particular shop, or encountering a certain person, which or whom he has reasons for wishing to avoid, will say to any friend who may be with him, I wish you'd stall me off from that crib, (or from that cove, as the case may be) meaning, walk in such a way as to cover or obscure me from notice, until we are past the shop or person in question.

STALL UP: To stall a person up, (a term used by pickpockets,) is to surround him in a crowd, or violent pressure, and even sometimes in the open street, while walking along, and by violence force his arms up, and keep them in that position while others of the gang rifle his pockets at pleasure, the cove being unable to help or defend himself; this is what the newspapers denominate hustling, and is universally practised at the doors of public theatres, at boxing matches, ship-launches, and other places where the general anxiety of all ranks, either to push forward, or to obtain a view of the scene before them, forms a pretext for jostling, and every other advantage which the strength or numbers of one party gives them over a weaker one, or a single person. It is not unusual for the buz-coves, on particular occasions, to procure a formidable squad of stout fellows of the lower class, who, though not expert at knuckling, render essential service by violently pushing and squeezing in the crowd, and, in the

A New and Comprehensive Vocabulary of the Flash Language

confusion excited by this conduct, the unconcerned prigs reap a plentiful harvest, and the stallers up are gratified with such part of the gains acquired, as the liberality of the knuckling gentlemen may prompt them to bestow. This coup de guerre is termed making a regular stall at such a place, naming the scene of their operations. See STALL.

STAMPS: shoes.

STAND THE PATTER. See PATTER'D.

STAR. The star is a game chiefly practised by young boys, often under ten years of age, although the offence is capital. It consists of cutting a pane of glass in a shop-window, by a peculiar operation called starring the glaze, which is performed very effectually by a common penknife; the depredators then take out such articles of value as lie within reach of their arm, which if they are not interrupted, sometimes includes half the contents of the window. A person convicted of this offence is said to have been done for a star.

START. See PITCHER.

STASH. To stash any practice, habit, or proceeding, signifies to put an end to, relinquish, or quash the same; thus, a thief determined to leave off his vicious courses will declare that he means to stash (or stow) prigging. A man in custody for felony, will endeavour, by offering money, or other means, to induce his prosecutor's forbearance, and compromise the matter, so as to obtain his liberation; this is called stashing the business. To stash drinking, card-playing, or any other employment you may be engaged in, for the time present, signifies to stow it, knife it, cheese it, or cut it, which are all synonymous, that is, to desist or leave off. See WANTED.

STASH IT. See STOW IT, which has the same meaning.

STAUNCH: a resolute faithful associate, in whom one may place implicit confidence, is said by his palls to be a staunch cover.

STEAMER: a tobacco-pipe.

STEVEN: money.

A New and Comprehensive Vocabulary of the Flash Language

STICK: a pistol.

STICKS: household furniture.

STING: to rob or defraud a person or place is called stinging them, as, that cove is too fly; he has been stung before; meaning that man is upon his guard; he has already been trick'd.

STINK: When any robbery of moment has been committed, which causes much alarm, or of which much is said in the daily papers, the family people will say, there is a great stink about it. See WANTED.

STONE-JUG; STONE-PITCHER: See PITCHER.

STOOP: the pillory is called the stoop; to be stoop'd, is to be set on the pillory.

STOOPING-MATCH: the exhibition of one or more persons on the pillory. See PUSH.

STOW: to stow any business, employment, or mode of life, is the same as to stash it, etc. See STASH.

STOW, STOW IT; or STOW FAKING: an intimation from a thief to his pall, to desist from what he is about, on the occasion of some alarm, etc. See AWAKE.

STOW, or STOW-MANGING: an intimation from one flash-cove to another in a mixed company to be silent, or drop the subject, he was upon. See MANG.

STOW THAT. When a person advances any assertion which his auditor believes to be false, or spoken in jest, or wishes the former to recant, the latter will say, stow that, if you please, or, cheese that, meaning don't say so, or that's out of the question.

STRETCH. Five or ten stretch, signifies five or ten yards, etc. ; so in dealing for any article, as linen, etc., I will give you three hog a stretch, means, I'll give three shillings a yard. See HOG.

STRING. See LINE.

A New and Comprehensive Vocabulary of the Flash Language

STRUMMEL: the hair of the head. To get your strummel faked in twig, is to have your hair dressed in style.

STUBBS: nothing.

SUIT: in general synonymous with game; as, what suit did you give it to 'em upon? in what manner did you rob them, or upon what pretence, etc., did you defraud them? One species of imposition is said to be a prime suit, another a queer suit: a man describing the pretext he used to obtain money from another, would say, I draw'd him if a quid upon the suit if so and so, naming the ground of his application. See DRAW. A person having engaged with another on very advantageous terms to serve or work for him, will declare that he is upon a good suit. To use great submission and respect in asking any favour of another, is called giving it to him upon the humble suit.

SWAG: a bundle, parcel, or package; as a swag of snow, etc. The swag, is a term used in speaking of any booty you have lately obtained, be it of what kind it may, except money, as Where did you lumber the swag? that is, where did you deposit the stolen property? To carry the swag is to be the bearer of the stolen goods to a place of safety. A swag of any thing, signifies emphatically a great deal. To have knap'd a good swag, is to have got a good booty.

SWAG. Wearing-apparel, linen, piece-goods, etc., are all comprehended under the name of swag, when describing any speak lately made, etc., in order to distinguish them from plate, jewellery, or other more portable articles.

SWELL: a gentleman; but any well-dressed person is emphatically termed a swell, or a rank swell. A family man who appears to have plenty of money, and makes a genteel figure, is said by his associates to be in swell street. Any thing remarkable for its beauty or elegance, is called a swell article; so a swell crib, is a genteel house; a swell mollisher, an elegantly-dressed woman, etc. Sometimes, in alluding to a particular gentleman, whose name is not requisite, he is styled, the swell, meaning the person who is the object of your discourse, or attention; and whether he is called the swell, the cove, or the gory, is immaterial, as in the following (in addition to many other) examples: I was turned up at China-street, because the swell would not appear; meaning, of course, the prosecutor: again, speaking of a person whom you were on the point of robbing, but who has taken the

A New and Comprehensive Vocabulary of the Flash Language

alarm, and is therefore on his guard, you will say to your pall, It's of no use, the cove is as down as a hammer; or, We may as well stow it, the gory's leary. See COVE and DOWN.

SWIMMER: a guard-ship, or tender; a thief who escapes prosecution, when before a magistrate, on condition of being sent on board the receiving-ship, to serve His Majesty, is said by his palls to be swimmered.

SWISH'D: married.

SWODDY, or SWOD-GILL: a soldier.

TANNER: a sixpence. Three and a tanner, is three and sixpence, etc.

TAT: to flog or scourge.

TATTS: dice.

TATT-BOX: a dice-box.

TATS AND ALL: an expression used out of flash, in the same manner as the word bender; and has a similar meaning.

TEAZE: to flog, or whip.

THIMBLE: a watch.

THIMBLED: having, or wearing a watch.

THRUMS, THRUMBUSKINS, or a THRUM-MOP: three pence.

THROUGH IT, or THROUGH THE PIECE: getting acquitted on an indictment, or surmounting any other trouble, or difficulty, is called getting through it, or thro' the piece; so, to get a man through it, etc., is to extricate him by virtue of your counsel and friendly assistance; sometimes called pulling him through it.

THROW OFF: to talk in a sarcastical strain, so as to convey offensive allusions under the mask of pleasantry, or innocent freedom; but, perhaps, secretly venting that abuse which you would not dare to give in direct terms; this is called throwing off, a practice at which the flash ladies are very expert, when any little jealousies arise

A New and Comprehensive Vocabulary of the Flash Language

among them. To begin to talk flash, and speak freely of robberies past, or in contemplation, when in company with family people, is also termed throwing off; meaning to banish all reserve, none but friends being present; also, to sing when called on by the company present. See CHAUNT.

TILBURY: a sixpence.

TINNY: a fire; a conflagration.

TINNY-HUNTERS: persons whose practice it is to attend fires, for the purpose of plundering the unfortunate sufferers, under pretence of assisting them to remove their property.

TIP: to give, pay, or bribe. To take the tip, is to receive a bribe in any shape; and they say of a person who is known to be corruptible, that he will stand the tip. The tip is a term frequently used to signify the money concerned in any dealings or contract existing between parties; synonymous with the dues. See DUES.

TITTER: a young woman or girl.

TOBY: to toby a man, is to rob him on the highway; a person convicted of this offence, is said to be done for a toby. The toby applies exclusively to robbing on horseback; the practice of footpad robbery being properly called the spice, though it is common to distinguish the former by the title of high-toby, and the latter of low-toby.

TOBY-GILL, or TOBY-MAN: properly signifies a highwayman.

TODDLE: to walk slowly, either from infirmity or choice. Come, let us toddle, is a familiar phrase, signifying, let us be going.

TODDLER: an infirm elderly person, or a child not yet perfect in walking.

TOG: a coat; to tog, is to dress or put on clothes; to tog a person, is also to supply them with apparel, and they are said to be well or queerly tog'd, according to their appearance.

TOG'D OUT TO THE NINES: a fanciful phrase, meaning simply, that a person is well or gaily dressed.

A New and Comprehensive Vocabulary of the Flash Language

TOGS, or TOGGERY: wearing-apparel in general.

TOM BRAY'S BILK: laying out ace and deuce at cribbage.

TOM BROWN: twelve in hand, or crib.

TOOLS: implements for house-breaking, picklocks, pistols, etc., are indiscriminately called the tools. A thief, convicted on the police act, of having illegal instruments or weapons about him, is said to be fined for the tools.

TOP: to top a clout or other article (among pickpockets) is to draw the corner or end of it to the top of a person's pocket, in readiness for shaking or drawing, that is, taking out, when a favourable moment occurs, which latter operation is frequently done by a second person.

TOP'D: hanged.

TO THE NINES; or, TO THE RUFFIAN. These terms are synonymous, and imply an extreme of any kind, or the superlative degree.

TOUT: to tout a person, is to watch his motions; to keep tout, is to look out, or watch, while your pall is effecting any private purpose. A strong tout, is a strict observation, or eye, upon any proceedings, or person.

TOW; or, TOWLINE. See LINE. To tow a person out; that is, from his premises, or post: is to decoy him therefrom by some fictitious story, or other artifice, while your pall seizes the opportunity of his absence, to rob the place he has imprudently quitted.

TRAPS: police officers, or runners, are properly so called; but it is common to include constables of any description under this title.

TRICK. See DO THE TRICK.

TRIG: a bit of stick, paper, etc., placed by thieves in the keyhole of, or elsewhere about, the door of a house, which they suspect to be uninhabited; if the trig remains unmoved the following day, it is a proof that no person sleeps in the house, on which the gang enter it the ensuing night upon the screw, and frequently meet with a good

A New and Comprehensive Vocabulary of the Flash Language

booty, such as beds, carpets, etc., the family being probably out of town. This operation is called trigging the jigger.

TRY IT ON: to make all attempt, or essay, where success is doubtful. So to try it on with a woman, signifies to attempt her chastity.

TURN UP: to desist from, or relinquish, any particular habit or mode of life, or the further pursuit of any object you had in view, is called turning it up. To turn up a mistress, or a male acquaintance, is to drop all intercourse, or correspondence, with them. To turn up a particular house, or shop, you have been accustomed to use, or deal at, signifies to withdraw your patronage, or custom, and visit it no more. To quit a person suddenly in the street, whether secretly or openly, is called turning him up. To turn a man up sweet, is to get rid of him effectually, but yet to leave him in perfect good humour, and free from any suspicion or discontent; this piece of finesse often affords a field for the exercise of consummate address, as in the case of turning up a flat, after having stript him of all his money at play, or a shopkeeper, whom you have just robbed before his face of something valuable, upon the pinch, or the hoist.

TURNED UP: a person acquitted by a jury, or discharged by a magistrate for want of evidence, etc., is said to be turned up. See SWELL.

TURNIPS: to give any body turnips signifies to turn him or her up, and the party so turned up, is said to have knap'd turnips.

TURN UP A TRUMP: to be fortunate in getting a good stake, or by any other means improving your finances.

TWIG: any thing accomplished cleverly, or as it should be, is said to be done in twig, in good twig, or in prime twig. A person well dress'd is said to be in twig. See DROP, GAMMON THE TWELVE, and OUT OF TWIG.

TWISTED: hanged.

TWO POLL ONE. See BRIDGE.

TYE IT UP: to tye up any particular custom, practice, or habit, is synonymous with knifeing, stowing, turning it up, or stashing it. To O'e it up is a phrase, which, used emphatically, is generally

A New and Comprehensive Vocabulary of the Flash Language

understood to mean a course of depredation and wickedness. See SQUARE, and DO THE TRICK.

UNBETTY: to unlock. See BETTY.

UNDUB: to unlock, unfasten, etc. See DUB UP.

UNPALLED: a thief whose associates are all apprehended, or taken from him by other means, is said to be unpalled, and he is then obliged to work single-handed.

UNSLOUR: to unlock, unfasten, or unbutton. See SLOUR. Speaking of a person whose coat is buttoned, so as to obstruct the access to his pockets, the knucks will say to each other, the cove is dour'd up, we must unslour him to get at his kickseys.

UNTHIMBLE: to unthimble a man, is to rob, or otherwise deprive him of his watch.

UNTHIMBLED: having been divested of one's watch.

UP IN THE STIRRUPS: a man who is in swell street, that is, having plenty of money, is said to be up in the stirrups.

UPON THE CROSS. See Cross.

UPON THE SQUARE. See SQUARE.

UPON THE SUIT, etc. See SUIT.

UPPER-BEN, UPPER-BENJAMIN, UPPER-TOG, a great-coat.

VARDO: a waggon.

VARDO-GILL: a waggoner.

WACK: to share or divide any thing equally, as wack the blunt, divide the money, etc.

WACK: a share or equal proportion, as give me my wack, that is, my due part.

A New and Comprehensive Vocabulary of the Flash Language

WALKER: an ironical expression, synonymous with bender, and used in the same manner.

WALKING-DISTILLER. See CARRY THE KEG.

WANTED: when any of the traps or runners have a private information against a family person, and are using means to apprehend the party, they say, such a one is wanted; and it becomes the latter, on receiving such intimation to keep out if the way, until the stink is over, or until he or she can find means to stash the business through the medium of Mr. Palmer, or by some other means.

WATER-SNEAK: robbing ships or vessels on a navigable river, or canal, by getting on board unperceived, generally in the night. The water-sneak, is lately made a capital offence.

WEAR IT: to wear it upon a person, (meaning to wear a nose, or a conk,) is synonymous with nosing, conking, splitting, or coming it, and is merely one of those fanciful variations so much admired by flash people.

WEAR THE BANDS. See BANDS.

WEDGE: silver; as a wedge-feeder, a silver spoon, etc. ; but silver coin, as well as silver plate, are both comprehended under the name of wedge. See RIDGE and SPEAK TO.

WEED: tobacco.

WEED: to pilfer or purloin a small portion from a large quantity of any thing; often done by young or timid depredators, in the hope of escaping detection, as, an apprentice or shopman will weed his master's lob, that is, take small sums out of the till when opportunity offers, which sort of peculation may be carried on with impunity for a length of time; but experienced thieves sometimes think it good Judgment to weed a place, in order that it may be good again, perhaps for a considerable length of time, as in the instance of a warehouse or other depot for goods, to which they may possess the means of access by means of a false key; in this ease, by taking too great a swag, at first, the proprietors would discover the deficiency, and take measures to prevent future depredation. To weed the swag is to embezzle part of the booty, unknown to your palls, before a

A New and Comprehensive Vocabulary of the Flash Language

division takes place, a temptation against which very few of tm family are proof, if they can find an opportunity. A flash-cove, on discovering a deficiency in his purse or property, which he cannot account for, will declare that he, (or it, naming the article,) has been weeded to the ruffian.

WEEDING DUES: speaking of any person, place, or property, that has been weeded, it is said weeding dues have been concerned. See DUES.

WEIGH FORTY: term used by the police, who are as well versed in flash as the thieves themselves. It is often customary with the traps, to wink at depredations of a petty nature, and for which no reward would attach, and to let a thief reign unmolested till he commits a capital crime. They then grab him, and, on conviction, share (in many cases) a reward of 40l., or upwards; therefore these gentry will say, Let him alone at present, we don't want him till he weighs his weight, meaning, of course, forty pounds.

WELL: to well your accomplice, or put him in the well, is explained under the word GARDEN, which see.

WHIDDLE: to speak of, or mention any thing, as, Don't you whiddle about so and so, that is, don't mention it.

WHIDDLER: a talkative or tell-tale person, who is not fit to be trusted with a secret.

WHIDS: words. See CRACK A WHID.

WHISTLERS. See BROWNS AND WHISTLERS.

WIN, or WINCHESTER: a penny.

WIND: a man transported for his natural life, is said to be lag'd for his wind, or to have knap'd a winder, or a bellowser, according to the humour of the speaker.

WOOLLY-BIRDS: sheep.

WORK. To work upon any particular game, is to practise generally, that species of fraud or depredation, as, He works upon the crack, he follows housebreaking, etc. An offender having been detected in the

A New and Comprehensive Vocabulary of the Flash Language

very fact, particularly in cases of coining, colouring base-metal, etc., is emphatically said to have been grab'd at work, meaning to imply, that the proof against him being so plain, he has no ground of defence to set up.

WRINKLE: to lie, or utter a falsehood.

WRINKLE: an untruth.

WRINKLER: a person prone to lying; such a character is called also a gully, which is probably an abbreviation of Gulliver, and from hence, to gully signifies to lie, or deal in the marvellous.

YACK: a watch (obsolete.)

YARN: yarning or spinning a yarn is a favourite amusement among flash-people; signifying to relate their various adventures, exploits, and escapes to each other. This is most common and gratifying, among persons in confinement or exile, to enliven a dull hour, and probably excite a secret hope of one day enjoying a repetition of their former pleasures. See BONED. A person expert at telling these stories, is said to spin a fine yarn. A man using a great deal of rhetoric, and exerting all his art to talk another person out of any thing he is intent upon, the latter will answer, Aye, Aye, you can spin a good yarn, but it won't do; meaning, all your eloquence will not have the desired effect.

YELLOW: jealous; a jealous husband is called a yellow gloak.

YOKUFF: a chest, or large box.

YORK: To stare or look at any person in an impertinent manner, is termed yorking; to york any thing, in a common sense, is to view, look at, or examine it.

YORK: a look, or observation; a flash-cove observing another person (a flat) who appears to notice or scrutinize him, his proceedings, or the company he is with, will say to his palls, That cove is yorking as strong as a horse, or, There is York-street concerned.

YOUKELL: a countryman, or clown.

A New and Comprehensive Vocabulary of the Flash Language

YOURNABS: yourself; an emphatical term used in speaking to another person.

FINIS.

Lightning Source UK Ltd.
Milton Keynes UK
UKOW02f1838220915

259104UK00001B/203/P